easy as cake

easy as cake

The Quickest Cakes, Cookies & Desserts You'll Ever Make

by Ruth Jolles

Photography by JOSEF SALIS

STERLING PUBLISHING CO., INC.
NEW YORK

Designed by Michel Opatowski
Edited by Ann Kleinberg
Food styling by Natasha Haimovich
Created by Penn Publishing Ltd.

Library of Congress Cataloging-in-Publication Data

Jolles, Ruth.
  Easy as . . . Cake / by Ruth Jolles ; photography by Josef Salis.
     p. cm.
  Includes index.
  ISBN 1-4027-1259-6
  1. Cake. 2. Baking. I. Title.

  TX771.Y647 2004
  641.8'653--dc22

                              2004056592

Library of Congress Cataloging-in-Publication Data

10   9   8   7   6   5   4   3   2   1

Published by Sterling Publishing Co., Inc.
387 Park Avenue South, New York, NY 10016
© 2005 by Penn Publishing Ltd.
Distributed in Canada by Sterling Publishing
$^c/o$ Canadian Manda Group, 165 Dufferin Street
Toronto, Ontario, Canada M6K 3H6
Distributed in Great Britain by Chrysalis Books Group PLC
The Chrysalis Building, Bramley Road, London W10 6SP, England
Distributed in Australia by Capricorn Link (Australia) Pty. Ltd.
P.O. Box 704, Windsor, NSW 2756, Australia

Sterling ISBN 1-4027-1259-6

Contents

A Word from the Author

I'm so glad you decided to roll up your sleeves, flour your counters, grease your hands, and get started on making your own cakes. I think you'll be surprised by how easy it is—and you'll definitely be delighted with the results.

Following the steps in this book, you'll become an expert on all kinds of cakes and desserts; even scones, popovers, and croissants will soon become part of your repertoire. There's a recipe for the best brownies you'll find anywhere and an apple and caramel cake that will make you think you're eating a tarte Tatin in a Paris bistro. When plums are in season, you'll be impressing friends with the delicious Summer Plum Cake, and when something exotic beckons, try the Pear and Pine Nuts Cake. There's German Coffee Cake, which is just right for late-afternoon tea, truffles for an after-dessert treat with coffee, and almond meringue cookies to whip up when those unexpected guests show up. Even when you think you have nothing on hand, I've got a cake for that too!

This is a book that will be fun to read and even more fun to follow. I hope you will feel really at home with these cakes—they come straight from my kitchen and my heart. They are part of a collection I've amassed over many years from family, friends, and many mothers, aunts, and grandmothers.

You don't have to be a genius in chemistry nor do you have to be an expert with a degree in baking to understand these recipes and make them work. They are straightforward, the instructions are clear, and nothing too sophisticated or pretentious is thrown in to confuse or frustrate you. I wrote this book to share my love of baking with you and I want you to enjoy it as much as I do.

In preparing the cakes for the beautiful photographs you'll see with each recipe, I had a Eureka! moment: Who is to say that you have to bake a cake in a specific pan? Why not try a large enamel mug instead of a springform pan or perhaps substitute several small heart-shaped pans for one large rectangular pan? The idea is to be creative, take the initiative, and make my cakes your cakes. Just remember to always use pans that are oven-proof (when baking is required) and never fill them more than three-fourths full.

The key to successful baking, in my opinion, is not to use shortcuts. These recipes are carefully planned, so please follow the directions. If the eggs should be at room temperature, make sure they are. If the butter needs to be softened before use, make sure it is. A cup is a measured cup, not like my mother's "just use the red wineglass" system. (It's no wonder her honey cake spilled out all over my oven.)

I've learned that it pays to use good equipment and of course the best ingredients. That is half the work. Before I send you on your way, I would like to say that I hope you'll fall in love with these recipes and adopt some favorites of your own so that they'll become a "specialty of the house" in your home. These are what your children and grandchildren will ask for— Mom's Orange Cake or Grandma's Brownies—when they make those nostalgic trips back home.

And if you are still wondering why to bother with all this baking fuss and not just buy ready-made from the supermarket, the answer is that there is nothing in the world as wonderful and comforting as the smell of a cake baking in the oven—except perhaps for the unforgettable taste. Go make a cake now and see for yourself!

—Ruth Jolles

Tips for Successful Baking

The following are some tips that I have gathered over many years of baking. They are very personal; no doubt each cook has his or her own methods that seem to work. My best advice to you is to use them only as a reference and to feel free to create your own. I would be very proud and happy to learn that you have adapted some of my ideas and improved upon them.

1. Prepare all the ingredients in advance on your work surface. Arrange them according to the order in which you will need them. Once this is done you have already accomplished half the work. Then all you have to do is pay attention to the recipe and follow the instructions.

2. Make sure you use the correct measuring cups and spoons. This is the Golden Rule of Baking. For liquids, it is highly recommended to use a Pyrex glass measuring cup. For dry or solid ingredients, a set of measuring cups is best. When measuring flour, spoon it into a dry measuring cup and level it off with a straight edge. Do not tap or shake the cup. A small scale would also be helpful in the kitchen.

3. Do not skimp on baking utensils and pans. The better the equipment, the better the results.

4. Look over the recipe again. After you have placed all the needed supplies on your work surface, look over the recipe again. If you forgot just one ingredient, you will be glad you checked.

5. Do not take shortcuts! Pay attention to instructions that require eggs to be at room temperature or softened butter.

6. Make sure that butter is sweet, not salted. In my career I have baked a few too many cakes that have come out salty.

7. It is advisable to first flour your hands when you are preparing cookies or working the dough with your hands. It makes it a lot easier to handle sticky dough.

8. Trying to loosen a cake from a pan while it is still warm can cause the cake to fall apart. Contrary to many baking books that recommend removing the cake from the oven and allowing it to cool for 15 minutes on a wire rack before removing it from the pan, I prefer to wait until the cake has completely cooled before releasing it from the pan. Even then I like to let it continue cooling on a wire rack. This will guarantee that the bottom of the cake is no longer moist.

9. Every oven is different, so it is important to know your oven. Use my temperatures as a guideline but keep in mind the parameters of your oven and adjust the heat accordingly.

10. When "sugar" is called for it means regular granulated sugar. Occasionally a recipe will specify confectioners' (powdered) or Demerara sugar.

11. Make sure cream is very cold before you whip it. You may even want to place the mixing bowl in the freezer for a short time before beating.

12. **Always sift together the flour, salt, and baking powder.** You can substitute cake flour if you prefer, but you will still need the baking powder.

13. **Use the best chocolate you can find when preparing chocolate cake.** It will make a big difference in the quality of the cake.

14. **Do not feel obligated to use the exact pans that I recommend.** Feel free to experiment with your own pans of different sizes and shapes. Just remember not to fill the pan more than ³/4 full with the batter. Instead of making one large cake, you can substitute two small pans. You might even consider using a planter instead of a pan (no kidding!) as long as it is made of a material that can be baked (and don't forget to cover the hole in the bottom). Try a large mug or a decorative ceramic bowl as long as it is tall enough and ovenproof. The idea is to have fun and be creative.

15. **Climate is one of the many factors that affect the success of a cake.** Pay attention to the results, and if there is a problem, try to figure out what caused it so that the next time you will be able to guarantee success. You may have to increase the baking time, add flour, or reduce the amount of liquid. Results are very individual, and I have learned that if you want to adapt recipes, you have to make them more than once and pay attention to varying conditions. Climate, oven temperature, age of ingredients, and even your mood affect the success of your baking.

16. **Try to use a commercially available spray that contains both oil and flour to grease and flour your pans.** You will not believe how easily the cakes slip out of the pans.

17. **Most cakes will freeze easily**, although I do not recommend freezing cheesecakes. The best way to serve them is to remove them from the freezer to defrost at room temperature, then place them in an oven preheated to 350° F for about 10 minutes.

18. **Some cakes (the noncreamy kinds) may dry out a bit after a day or two.** This is the perfect opportunity to toast the slices and serve them warm with fresh butter. It's a wonderful treat, especially with lemon, orange, and butter cakes.

19. **I love to add unusual spices to my cakes.** Try, for example, candied ginger, grated lemon peel, or even rosemary. I often substitute almond instead of vanilla extract, especially in chocolate cakes. Try a liqueur other than the one specified in the recipe. Instead of walnuts or pecans, consider using pine nuts or pistachios. Use my recipes as guidelines and experiment, but remember that you will no doubt be very happy with the results when you have succeeded with an idea of your own.

20. **You can upgrade a cake by decorating it.** I like to use fresh or small silk flowers, or sometimes I sift confectioners' sugar over the cake in a pattern. Try garnishing with a small lemon, tiny oranges with a few leaves still attached, or even a few mint sprigs. The effort is small but the results can be spectacular.

Sour Cream
& Cheesecakes

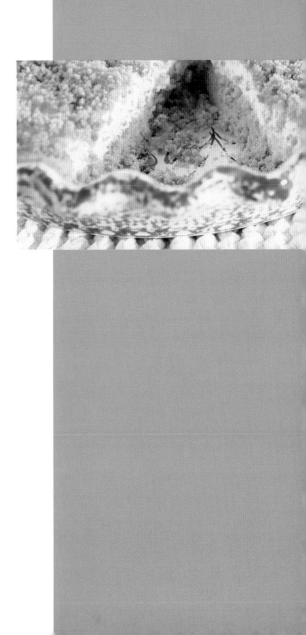

Cheesecake with Petit Beurre Crust

A delicious cheesecake that is perfect for any occasion.
Best if prepared one day in advance.

10-inch springform pan,
greased

10 ounces
petit beurre biscuits
or **honey-flavored graham
crackers**

6 tablespoons
butter, room temperature

2 (8-ounce) packages
cream cheese, room
temperature

2 large **eggs**

1 cup **sugar**

2 tablespoons **cornstarch**

1 cup **whipping cream**

2 cups **sour cream**

1
Preheat oven to 220°F.
In a food processor fitted with the steel blade, grind the biscuits
until fine. Combine with the butter and mix together well.
Press the mixture onto the bottom and up the sides of the
prepared pan.

2
In a large mixing bowl, beat the cream cheese, eggs, and $1/2$ cup
sugar until blended. Gradually add the cornstarch. Pour the batter
onto the crumb layer and bake for 20 minutes. Remove from
oven and let stand for 10 minutes.

3
Beat the whipping cream until it forms soft peaks. Add the sour
cream and the remaining $1/2$ cup sugar and continue to mix for an
additional 3 minutes. Pour on top of the cooled cake, return to
oven, and bake for an additional 20 minutes.

4
Remove cake from oven even though it is still white and a bit
loose. Let cool, release the sides of the pan, and store in
refrigerator until the next day.

Sour Cream Cake

The rich flavor of sour cream combined with vanilla makes this cake a joy to eat. The batter is baked in two pans: one for the crust and one for the crumb topping. Best if prepared one day in advance.

10-inch springform pan and another **smaller pan** (for the crumbs), both greased

BATTER:

¾ cup **butter**, room temperature

2 cups **all-purpose flour**

2 teaspoons **baking powder**

2 small **eggs**

⅓ cup **sugar**

FILLING:

½ cup **butter**, room temperature

3 large **eggs**

1 teaspoon **vanilla extract**

½ cup **sugar**

2 cups **sour cream**

1

Preheat oven to 400°F.

Combine all the batter ingredients in a bowl and mix until well blended.

Transfer ³/₄ of the batter to the springform pan and press mixture firmly onto the bottom and up the sides.

Place the remainder of the batter in the smaller pan and press onto the bottom.

Place both pans in the oven and bake for 25 to 30 minutes, until the crust is deep golden.

Remove and let cool.

2

Beat together all the filling ingredients except for the sour cream. When well-blended, add the sour cream and mix with a spoon.

3

Pour the filling into the cooled springform crust.

Crumble the mixture from the smaller pan with your hands and sprinkle evenly over the filling.

Chill overnight.

Cheesecake
with Sour Cream Topping

10-inch springform pan, greased

BATTER:

1¾ cups crushed **petit beurre biscuits** or **honey-flavored graham crackers**

¾ cup **butter**, room temperature

FILLING:

4 large **eggs**

1 cup **sugar**

1½ pounds **ricotta cheese**

1 teaspoon **vanilla extract**

juice of **½** lemon

TOPPING:

2 cups **sour cream**

1

Preheat oven to 300°F.

In a large bowl, combine the crushed biscuits and the butter with your hands.

Press mixture onto the bottom and up the sides of the prepared pan.

2

In a mixer, beat the filling ingredients until blended.

Pour mixture over the crushed biscuits.

Bake for 30 minutes and then remove from oven.

(Cake will be baked additionally after topping is added.)

3

Carefully spread the sour cream on top of the baked cake.

Return to oven and bake for additional 15 minutes.

Remove from oven, let cool, then chill for at least 4 hours.

Meringue Cheesecake

This is a lovely cake with a very delicate taste and no crust.

10-inch springform pan, greased

2 (8-ounce) packages **cream cheese**, room temperature

1 cup **sour cream**

1 cup **sugar**

4 large **eggs** (1 whole, 3 separated), room temperature

½ teaspoon **vanilla extract**

1 tablespoon **lemon juice**

grated **peel** of **1 lemon**

2 heaping tablespoons **all-purpose flour**

½ teaspoon **baking powder**

1

Preheat oven to 350°F.

In a large bowl, beat the cream cheese, sour cream, ³/4 cup sugar, 1 whole egg, 3 egg yolks, vanilla, lemon juice, grated lemon peel, flour, and baking powder for 3 to 4 minutes.

Pour mixture into the prepared pan and bake for 20 minutes.

2

In a clean, dry bowl, beat the 3 egg whites until they form soft peaks. Gradually add the remaining ¹/4 cup sugar, 1 tablespoon at a time, and continue to beat until stiff and glossy. (This forms the meringue.)

3

Remove cake from oven and spread meringue on top.

Bake for an additional 20 minutes, or until the cake turns light golden.

4

Remove from oven, let cool, then chill for several hours.

Cheesecake with Crumb Topping

This is a wonderful cheesecake with a surprise layer of jam. Best if chilled overnight and served the next day.

10-inch springform pan and another **smaller pan** (for the crumbs), both greased

BATTER:

1 cup **butter**, room temperature

2 egg yolks

2 teaspoons **baking powder**

2 tablespoons **sugar**

2 cups **all-purpose flour**

2 tablespoons **strawberry** or **apricot jam**

FILLING:

2 (8-ounce) packages **cream cheese**, room temperature

3/4 cup **sugar**

1 teaspoon **vanilla extract**

1 cup **whipping cream**

2 tablespoons **sugar**

1

Preheat oven to 350°F.
Place all the batter ingredients except the jam in a food processor fitted with the steel blade and pulse until combined. Press one half of the mixture onto the bottom and up the sides of the larger springform pan. Press the remaining batter onto the bottom of the smaller pan. Bake both for 20 minutes, or until the crust is deep golden.

2

Remove from oven and spread the jam on the top of the baked crust in the larger pan.

3

Beat the cream cheese with the 3/4 cup sugar and vanilla. In another mixing bowl, beat the whipping cream until soft peaks form. Add the 2 tablespoons sugar, beat for another few minutes, and fold into the cheese mixture. Using a spatula, transfer the cheese mixture into the large pan on top of the jam layer.

4

Using your fingers, crumble the crust from the smaller pan and sprinkle over the cheesecake. Chill overnight.

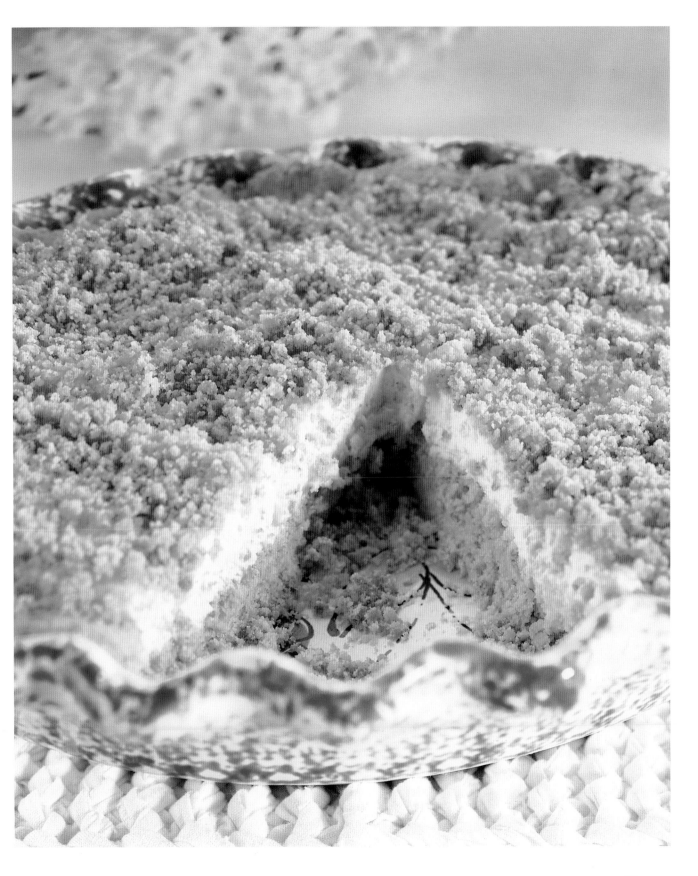

Two-Tone Chocolate Cheesecake

The highlight of your Sunday brunch! With the appearance of marble cake and the texture of pound cake, your guests will probably be surprised to discover that this is a cheesecake.
Light enough to have with coffee for breakfast, it's also perfect served with hot tea after a main dessert.

9½ x 5½ x 3¼ -inch loaf **pan**, greased

¾ cup coarsely chopped **bittersweet chocolate**

1 cup **butter**, room temperature

4 large **eggs**

1 cup **sugar**

1 teaspoon **vanilla extract**

3 cups **all-purpose flour**

3 teaspoons **baking powder**

1¼ cups (10 ounces) **cream cheese**, room temperature

1
Preheat oven to 350°F.
In a saucepan over low heat, melt the chocolate with the butter.

2
In a mixing bowl or food processor fitted with the steel blade, mix all the remaining ingredients.
Pour half of the mixture into the prepared pan.
Mix the remaining half with the chocolate and pour it over the first layer.

3
Bake for 40 to 45 minutes, or until a cake tester inserted in the center comes out clean.

Chocolate
Cakes

Ultimate Chocolate Cake

A wonderful chocolate cake that gets even better the next day. It can keep for a week unrefrigerated and also stays great in the freezer.

10-inch springform pan, greased and floured

1 cup **butter**

1 cup **milk**

1½ cups **sugar**

3 tablespoons **unsweetened cocoa**

1 teaspoon **instant coffee powder**

7 ounces **bittersweet** or **semisweet chocolate**, broken into pieces

4 large **eggs**, separated, room temperature

1¼ cups **all-purpose flour**

1¼ teaspoons **baking powder**

1

Preheat oven to 350°F.

In a saucepan over medium heat, melt butter with milk, sugar, cocoa, coffee, and chocolate, stirring constantly until smooth. Pour the mixture into a bowl and add the egg yolks, one at a time, stirring well.

2

Measure out 1 cup of mixture and set aside for use as frosting.

3

Beat the egg whites until they form stiff peaks.

Sift together the flour and baking powder.

Fold the flour mixture into the chocolate mixture and then fold in the beaten egg whites.

Pour the batter into the prepared pan and bake for 45 minutes, or until a cake tester inserted in the center comes out clean.

Remove from oven, spread with the reserved frosting, and let cool.

Note: This cake can also be made in a rectangular baking pan and served as individual squares. Elegant when served with sliced almonds scattered over the top.

Very Easy Chocolate Cake

You will not believe something this easy could be so delicious! It's perfect to keep on the kitchen counter for "starving" children, grazing spouses, or unexpected company, and it goes well with just about anything: try serving it warm with ice cream, fruit soup, or syrup, or even icing and decorating it.

10-inch springform pan, greased and floured

1 cup **butter**

5 ounces **bittersweet chocolate**, broken into pieces

1 cup **sugar**

1½ cups **all-purpose flour**

1½ teaspoons **baking powder**

4 large **eggs**

½ cup **milk**

1

Preheat oven to 350°F.

In a saucepan over low heat, melt the butter with the chocolate and sugar, stirring constantly until smooth. Remove from heat. Add the flour, baking powder, eggs, and milk and stir with a wooden spoon until blended.

2

Pour batter into the prepared pan and bake for 45 minutes, or until a cake tester inserted in the center comes out clean.

Frosted Chocolate Cake

Rich, moist, positively sinful—this is the chocolate lover's dream cake. You can use the delectable frosting on many of the other cakes in this book as well . . . if you can resist eating it all by itself, that is. This cake is ideal for birthdays or for any other happy occasion.

10-inch springform or **rectangular pan**, greased and floured

BATTER:

2 large **eggs**

1¼ cups **sugar**

1 cup **canola oil**

1 teaspoon **vanilla extract**

1 cup **boiling water**

2 cups **all-purpose flour**

2 level teaspoons **baking powder**

1¼ cups **sweetened cocoa powder**

FROSTING:

4 ounces **bittersweet chocolate**

½ cup **whipping cream**

1

Preheat oven to 350°F.

Beat together the eggs and sugar.

Add the oil, vanilla, boiling water, flour, baking powder, and cocoa, and continue to beat until blended.

Pour into the prepared pan and bake for 45 minutes, or until a cake tester inserted in the center comes out clean.

2

Melt the chocolate and cream in a saucepan over medium heat, stirring constantly until smooth.

While still warm, spread over the warm cake with a spatula. (It will thicken as it cools.)

Brownies

The best brownies ever!

8-inch square glass pan, greased and floured

1 cup **butter**

3½ ounces **best quality unsweetened chocolate**

3 tablespoons **dark unsweetened cocoa**

1½ cups **all-purpose flour**

½ teaspoon **baking powder**

1 teaspoon **salt**

4 large **eggs**, room temperature

2 cups **sugar**

1 teaspoon **vanilla extract**

1½ cups **semisweet chocolate chips**

¾ cup **pecans** (or walnuts or eliminate the nuts), chopped

1

Preheat oven to 350°F.

Melt the butter and chocolate in the top of a double boiler, stirring occasionally, until smooth.

Set aside to cool.

2

Sift together the cocoa, flour, baking powder, and salt and set aside.

Beat eggs and gradually add the sugar, beating after each addition.

Add vanilla and cooled chocolate-butter mixture.

Stir in sifted dry ingredients just until combined.

Do not overmix!

3

Spread batter into prepared pan.

Sprinkle chips and nuts evenly over top.

Bake for 30 minutes, or until center no longer jiggles when shaken.

Insert a cake tester or toothpick in center to check that it comes out clean.

Remove immediately. *Do not overbake!*

Freezer Cakes
& Desserts

Chocolate Freezer Cheesecake

This cake is perfect to keep frozen for emergencies. It always tastes great, even after a long time in the freezer. The ultimate crowd-pleaser when served bite-size in individual paper cups.

---

13 x 9 x 2-inch freezer-proof pan

20 chocolate graham crackers

1 cup less **2** tablespoons **butter**

7 ounces **bittersweet** or **semisweet chocolate**

¼ cup **water**

4 large **eggs**, separated, room temperature

1 cup (8 ounces) **cream cheese**, room temperature

1 teaspoon **vanilla extract**

¾ cup **sugar**

1
Line the pan with 10 whole graham crackers.

2
In a saucepan over low heat, combine the butter, chocolate, and water; stir until melted.
Remove from heat and transfer to a mixing bowl.
While stirring constantly, gradually add the egg yolks, cream cheese, and vanilla; stir until blended.

3
In another mixing bowl, beat the egg whites until they start to stiffen. Gradually add the sugar, 1 tablespoon at a time, and continue beating until stiff and glossy.

4
Fold the beaten egg white mixture into the chocolate mixture.
Pour half of the mixture over the graham cracker layer.
Cover with another layer of graham crackers.
Pour in remaining mixture.
Cover with aluminum foil or plastic food wrap and freeze for several hours before serving.

Halvah Cake

Halvah (candy made from ground sesame and honey) gives this cake an exotic flavor. It is readily available, if not at local supermarkets then at Middle Eastern and specialty food shops.

10½-inch round cake pan, bottom and sides lined with plastic food wrap, or use 6 individual dishes

6 large **eggs**, separated, room temperature

dash of **salt**

²/₃ cup **sugar**

2 cups **whipping cream**

14 ounces **vanilla-flavored halvah**

1

Beat the egg whites until they form soft peaks. Add the salt and continue to beat. Gradually add $1/2$ cup of the sugar, 1 tablespoon at a time, and continue to beat until stiff and glossy.

2

In a large bowl, beat the yolks with the remaining sugar until the mixture turns light yellow.
In another bowl, beat the whipping cream until stiff peaks form.

3

Using your fingers or a fork, crumble the halvah and sprinkle it over the yolk mixture. Carefully fold in the egg white mixture and then the whipped cream. Using a spatula, transfer the mixture to the plastic-lined pan and freeze.
Before serving, remove from freezer and invert onto serving plate.

Praline Cake

This sweet, nutty cake is made with honey-roasted pecans, also known as "Chinese" or "sweetened" pecans. You can easily substitute sugared almonds. Both nuts are available in supermarkets, Middle Eastern, and specialty food shops.

2 (9½ x 5½ x 3¼-inch) loaf **pans**, lined with plastic food wrap

1½ cups **honey-roasted pecans**

2 cups **whipping cream**

3 tablespoons **sugar**

12 **meringue cookies** (white, 2 inches in diameter)

2 tablespoons **butter**

½ cup sliced **almonds**

1 In a food processor fitted with the steel blade, coarsely chop the pecans.

2 In a mixing bowl, beat the whipping cream until it forms soft peaks . Add 1 tablespoon sugar and beat for another minute. Crumble up the cookies and mix in with the whipping cream. Add the pecans.

3 Melt the butter with the remaining 2 tablespoons sugar. Add the almonds and sauté until browned. Let cool.

4 Divide the almonds and line the bottom of the two pans with them. Pour the batter over them, cover with plastic food wrap, and place in freezer overnight.
Before serving, invert onto serving plate and peel off plastic wrap.

Note: To make your own sweetened pecans, you will need 1 cup pecans, $^1/_2$ cup sugar, and vegetable oil for deep-frying.

Place the pecans in a strainer and wash well. Place in bowl and combine with the sugar using your fingers. Cover with plastic wrap and chill overnight. Remove from refrigerator and deep-fry in batches for about 3 minutes. (Make sure they don't burn; reduce heat if necessary.) Pecans are light brown when they are ready. Remove pecans from pan with a slotted spoon and drain. Can be stored in the freezer for up to three months.

Hazelnut Cream Cake

You can even serve this cake as a mousse: just eliminate the ladyfingers, pour the batter into champagne glasses, and chill.

10-inch springform pan, ungreased

2 teaspoons **instant coffee powder**

2 teaspoons **sugar**

1 cup **water**

20 ladyfingers (preferably the long imported ones)

7 ounces **hazelnuts** (unsalted, roasted and peeled)

2 cups **whipping cream**

1 can **sweetened condensed milk**

2 tablespoons **confectioners' sugar**

hazelnuts, chopped, for decoration

1

Dissolve the coffee powder and sugar in $^1/_4$ cup warm water. Add $^3/_4$ cup cold water. Pour the coffee into a small flat container. Break 10 ladyfingers in half, leaving the rest whole. Carefully dip all the ladyfingers into the coffee. Use the whole ones to cover the bottom of the pan and the halved ones to stand up along the sides of the pan (cut side down). *Be careful not to soak up too much of the coffee or the ladyfingers will fall apart.*

2

In a food processor fitted with the steel blade, process the hazelnuts for approximately 5 minutes, until they take on the consistency of soft peanut butter.
In a mixing bowl beat the whipping cream until it forms soft peaks. Reduce the speed of the mixer and gradually add the condensed milk, powdered sugar, and hazelnut butter.

3

Spread mixture evenly in the pan using a spatula. Cover with plastic food wrap and place in freezer overnight.
When ready to serve, loosen and remove the sides of the springform pan and place cake on a serving dish. (The bottom part of the pan can stay underneath the cake.) Decorate with the chopped hazelnuts.

Red Plum Sorbet

Keep this on hand in the freezer. Serve a scoop with a brownie decorated with confectioners' sugar and garnish with a fresh mint leaf. It takes a bit of effort, but the results are worth it.

8½ x 4½ x 2¾-inch loaf pan, lined with plastic food wrap

13 Santa Rosa (large red) plums, pitted

6 cups **water**

1½ cups **sugar**

1 teaspoon **vanilla extract**

grated **peel** of **1 lemon**

¼ cup **lemon juice**

2 tablespoons **Grand Marnier** or other **orange liqueur**

1

In a saucepan over medium heat, combine all the ingredients and bring to a boil.

Reduce heat and cook at a simmer until the plums have softened. Remove the plums with a slotted spoon and reserve the liquid.

2

In a food processor fitted with the steel blade, puree the plums. Add the reserved liquid and mix together well.

Pour the mixture into the prepared pan, cover with plastic food wrap, and freeze for at least 10 hours.

3

Remove from freezer and puree in a food processor. Transfer mixture to lined loaf pan and freeze again for 5 hours. Remove, puree once again, and freeze for 3 hours.

Chocolate Mousse

Unbelievably easy to make, this dessert is rich, elegant, and never boring. Try mixing your favorite chopped nuts or fruit directly into the mousse for endless variety. For a really spectacular look, serve in a champagne glass garnished with fresh mint leaves and fruit or drizzled with fruit syrup.

6 champagne or **wineglasses**

3 cups **whipping cream**

13 ounces **Nutella** chocolate spread

½ cup **chopped almonds** or **fresh berries,** for decoration

1

In an electric mixer on high speed, beat the cream until it forms soft peaks.

Reduce the speed and add the Nutella. Continue to beat until mixture forms a mousse.

Divide among the glasses and chill for several hours.

2

Before serving, decorate with the chopped almonds or fresh berries.

Tip: If the Nutella is too hard to whip, place in the microwave and soften. (Don't forget to remove the gold liner first.)

Passion Fruit Mousse

When passion fruit is in season, this makes a delicious and unusual dessert. It invites the creative to add exotic, colorful garnish and can be frozen in an endless variety of shapes and sizes. Passion fruit isn't a flavor most people get to enjoy every day, so be sure to make enough for those passionate palates!

bundt pan, molded gelatin ring, or **8½ x 4½ x 2¾-inch loaf pan**, lined with plastic food wrap

2 cups **whipping cream**

4 tablespoons **confectioners' sugar**

10 large **passion fruit** (or 15 small)

edible flowers, for garnish

1

Beat the cream until it forms soft peaks. Add the sugar and continue beating until stiff.

Cut each passion fruit in half and remove the pulp.

Mix the pulp into the cream mixture and combine well.

2

Pour mixture into the prepared pan, cover with plastic food wrap, and freeze.

Remove from freezer 15 minutes before serving. Remove plastic food wrap, invert onto serving plate, and peel off bottom layer of food wrap.

Slice and serve garnished with edible flowers.

Mango Sorbet

9½ x 5½ x 3½-inch loaf **pan**, lined with plastic food wrap

1 cup **sugar**

1½ cups **water**

¼ cup **fresh lemon juice**

3 large **mangoes** (or 4 medium), peeled and cubed

1

In a saucepan over medium heat, bring the sugar and water to a boil and cook until the sugar has melted.
Remove from heat and bring to room temperature.

2

In a food processor fitted with the steel blade, or a blender, puree the mangoes.
Strain the puree over a bowl using a sieve or food grinder to filter out little pieces.
Mix the strained mango liquid with the lemon juice and combine well with the cooled sugar water.
Pour into the prepared pan and freeze for at least 6 hours.

3

Remove the mango mixture from the freezer, break into pieces, and puree again.
Pour back into lined pan, cover with plastic food wrap, and freeze until ready to serve.

4

Just before serving, remove from freezer. Remove cover and invert onto serving plate. Peel off plastic lining, slice, and serve.
Garnish with fresh mangoes, mint leaves, or pomegranate seeds, if you like.

Fruit Cakes

Apple Patchwork Pie

A cake that sounds complicated but is really quite easy. The crust need not be in one piece and that's the beauty of it. The end result will look like a wonderful patchwork quilt.

9-inch springform or **pie pan**, greased

DOUGH:

½ cup **butter**, room temperature

½ cup granulated **sugar**

dash of **salt**

1 large **egg**, room temperature

1 ¾ cups **all-purpose flour**

1 teaspoon **vanilla extract**

1 tablespoon **bread crumbs**

FILLING:

4 large **Granny Smith** or **Braeburn apples**

¼ cup **sugar**

juice of ½ **lemon**

1½ tablespoons **all-purpose flour**

½ tablespoon **cinnamon**

dash of **ground nutmeg**

3 tablespoons **butter**, cut into cubes

1½ tablespoons **confectioners' sugar**

1

In a food processor fitted with the steel blade, combine the butter, granulated sugar, salt and egg. Add the flour and vanilla extract and continue to mix until it becomes a ball.
Cover with plastic food wrap and chill for several hours.

2

Remove dough from refrigerator and let rest for about 30 minutes, until it reaches room temperature. Divide the dough into two equal portions.

3

Put one portion on a clean, floured work surface and roll it out with a floured rolling pin to a circle 10½ inches in diameter and ¼ inch thick. Using a spatula, scoop up portions of the dough (it's okay if it breaks into large sections) and place in the prepared pan, covering the bottom and the sides. Sprinkle with the bread crumbs.

4

Peel, core, and slice the apples. Combine with the sugar, lemon juice, and flour and spread on top of the dough in the pan. Sprinkle cinnamon and nutmeg on top and cover with the butter cubes.
(As an interesting flavor option, add 1 tablespoon sugared ginger candies.)

5

Preheat oven to 350°F. Flatten out the remaining

portion of dough to a circle 9 inches in diameter, and repeat the process of scooping portions with a spatula and laying them on top of the filling.

Bake for 45 minutes, or until the dough turns golden brown. If using a springform pan, wait until it's cool before removing the sides.

6

Before serving, sprinkle with confectioners' sugar sifted through a fine-mesh sieve.

Comfort Apple Cake

Apart from the raisins I added to this recipe (you don't want to leave them out!), this is a traditional apple cake that will remind you of the coziness of Grandma's kitchen. Ideal for a cold winter day, it fills the house with a wonderful aroma and is irresistible served with hot tea, cider, or vanilla ice cream and whipped cream.

10-inch springform pan, greased and floured

2 pounds Granny Smith or **Braeburn apples**

½ teaspoon **cinnamon**

1 cup plus **1** tablespoon **sugar**

1 cup **all-purpose flour**

1 teaspoon **baking powder**

½ cup **canola oil**

3 large **eggs**, room temperature

½ cup **golden raisins**

1

Preheat oven to 350°F.

Peel, core, and coarsely grate the apples. Place in the bottom of the prepared pan.

Sprinkle with the cinnamon and 1 tablespoon sugar.

2

In a mixer, combine the flour, baking powder, remaining 1 cup sugar, oil, eggs, and raisins. Pour the batter over the apple slices in the pan.

Bake for 30 minutes, or until the cake turns golden.

Serve warm, scooped out with a large spoon.

Apple Crumb Cake

10-inch springform pan,
greased

DOUGH:

¾ cup **butter**, room
temperature

2¼ cups **all-purpose flour**

2¼ teaspoons **baking powder**

2 tablespoons **sugar**

2 large **egg yolks**

2 tablespoons **sour cream**

1 tablespoon **fresh lemon
juice**

FILLING:

2 pounds **Granny Smith** or
Braeburn apples

4 tablespoons **sugar**

1 tablespoon **cinnamon**

½ cup **pecans,** coarsely
chopped

1

In a food processor fitted with the steel blade, combine all the dough ingredients and pulse until well blended.
Press two-thirds of the dough onto the bottom and sides of the greased pan.
Chill the remaining dough for 10 minutes.

2

Preheat oven to 350°F.
Peel and coarsely grate the apples.
Gently squeeze out the excess water with your hands.
Divide the apples in two and spoon one part over the dough in the pan.

3

Mix the sugar, cinnamon, and pecans together and sprinkle half the amount over the apples.
Cover with the remaining apples and sprinkle with the rest of the sugar, cinnamon, and nut mixture.

4

Remove the chilled dough from the refrigerator and coarsely grate it over the nuts. (This forms the crumb topping.)
Bake for 45 minutes, or until the cake turns golden.

Apple and Caramel Cake

There's nothing like an apple cake to soothe the soul. This one is especially delicious when eaten on a cold wintry night next to the fireplace, but it's great to enjoy in the summertime too.
If you like tarte Tatin, you'll love this!

10-inch springform pan, greased

DOUGH:

½ cup **butter**, room temperature

5 tablespoons **granulated sugar**

1 teaspoon **vanilla extract**

1½ cups all-purpose flour

FILLING:

8 large **Granny Smith** or **Braeburn apples**

6 tablespoons **butter**

¾ cup **brown sugar**

grated **peel** of **1 lemon**

1 teaspoon **vanilla extract**

1

In a food processor fitted with the steel blade, combine the butter, sugar, vanilla, and flour and puree until the dough takes on a crumbly texture. Divide the batter in two; put one half aside and press the other half into the prepared pan. (Flatten it out like a tart.)

2

Preheat oven to 350°F.
Peel, core, and cut the apples into eighths.
Combine with the other filling ingredients in a saucepan and cook over medium heat for 30 minutes, stirring occasionally. Cook until the liquids have evaporated and the apples take on a caramel coating.

3

Pour the apple mixture into the prepared pan and cover with the remaining dough.
Bake for 55 minutes, or until the cake starts to bubble and turn golden.

Applesauce Cake

No fresh apples on hand? Not to worry. With just a jar of unsweetened applesauce you can still make a great cake.

10-inch springform pan, greased

1½ cups **sugar**

½ cup **vegetable oil**

2 large **eggs**, room temperature

2½ cups **all-purpose flour**

2½ teaspoons **baking powder**

½ teaspoon **salt**

1 teaspoon **cinnamon**

½ teaspoon **ground nutmeg**

1¼ cups **unsweetened applesauce**

1 teaspoon **baking soda**

½ cup **boiling water**

1
Preheat oven to 350°F.
In a mixing bowl or food processor fitted with the steel blade, mix the sugar and oil until blended.
Add in the eggs one at a time, beating until blended after each addition.

2
Combine the flour, baking powder, salt, cinnamon, and nutmeg.
Add the dry ingredients alternately with the applesauce to the sugar and oil mixture, beginning and ending with the dry ingredients, until well blended.

3
Dissolve the baking soda in the boiling water and add to the batter; mix well.
Pour the mixture into the prepared pan.
If you'd like, decorate the top of the cake with thinly sliced fresh apples.
Bake for 45 minutes, or until the cake starts to brown.

Banana Cake

A great idea when you have overripe bananas in the house. Perfect for a weekend brunch, the cake stays fresh for at least a week if covered with aluminum foil. (This recipe makes two cakes.)

---

2 (9½ x 5½ x 3 ¼-inch) loaf pans, greased and floured

½ cup **butter**, room temperature

1 ½ cups **sugar**

2 large **eggs**, room temperature

1 teaspoon **vanilla extract**

¼ cup **buttermilk** (or yogurt or sour cream)

2 cups **all-purpose flour**

½ teaspoon **baking powder**

⅓ teaspoon **baking soda**

½ teaspoon **salt**

1 cup mashed **ripe bananas** (about 2 large ones)

1

Preheat oven to 350°F.
In a mixing bowl, combine the butter, sugar, eggs, and vanilla and beat for 2 minutes.
Add the buttermilk and mix well.

2

In another bowl, sift together the flour, baking powder, baking soda, and salt.

3

Slowly add the dry ingredients alternately with the mashed bananas to the butter and sugar mixture; stir until mixed. Pour the batter into the two prepared pans and bake for 30 minutes, or until a cake tester inserted in the center comes out clean.

Lemon Cake

This cake takes on the most delicious flavor when lemons
are at their freshest.

9¹⁄₂ x 5¹⁄₂ x 3¹⁄₄-inch loaf
pan, greased and floured

4 large **eggs**, room
temperature

1¹⁄₃ cups **sugar**

pinch of **salt**

grated **peel** of **3** large **lemons**

1³⁄₄ cups **all-purpose flour**

1³⁄₄ teaspoons **baking powder**

¹⁄₂ cup **whipping cream**

6 tablespoons **butter**, melted
and brought to room
temperature

1

Preheat oven to 350°F.
In a mixer, beat the eggs, sugar and salt until the mixture is light
yellow. Beat in the grated lemon peel.

2

In another bowl, mix the flour and baking powder.
Sift one third of the flour mixture into the egg mixture and mix
well.
Sift another third of the flour mixture into the batter, mix well,
then sift the final third in and continue mixing.
Beat in the whipping cream.
Add the butter and blend well.

3

Pour batter into pan and bake for 45 minutes or until cake tester
inserted in the center comes out clean.
Remove from oven and cool on wire rack.

Pear and Pine Nut Cake

This cake is best with fresh pears, but if they're not available use well-drained canned ones. The pine nuts add a wonderful Italian accent.

10½-inch springform pan, greased and floured

1 cup **butter**, room temperature

1½ cups **sugar**

4 large **eggs**, room temperature

2½ cups **all-purpose flour**

2½ teaspoons **baking powder**

1½ pounds small, soft **pears**, peeled, cored, and halved

½ cup **pine nuts**

2 tablespoons **demerara sugar,** for decorating

1

Preheat oven to 350°F.

In a large mixing bowl, beat the butter and sugar together until the mixture becomes light yellow.

Add the eggs, one at a time, beating well after each addition.

2

Sift the flour and baking powder together over the egg mixture and stir in.

Pour the batter into the prepared pan and smooth the top.

Arrange the pears (cut side down) in a circle around the edge.

Create smaller and smaller circles inside it until you reach the center and the batter is covered.

Scatter the pine nuts over the pears.

3

Bake for 50 to 60 minutes, until the top starts to turn golden and a cake tester inserted in the center comes out clean.

Remove from oven and let cool for 10 minutes on a wire rack.

Sprinkle with demerara sugar and release from pan.

Continue cooling. Wonderful served with crème fraîche.

Blueberry Crumb Cake

If fresh blueberries are not available, use frozen or canned, well-drained.

9-inch springform or
round cake pan or
**9½ x 5½ x 3 ¼-inch loaf
pan**, greased and floured.

CRUMB TOPPING:

¼ cup **butter**, cold

½ cup granulated **sugar**

⅓ cup **all-purpose flour**

½ teaspoon **cinnamon**

BATTER:

2 cups **all-purpose flour**

2 teaspoons **baking powder**

3 large **eggs**, room
temperature

¾ cup **granulated sugar**

¼ cup **butter**, room
temperature

¾ cup **milk**

¼ teaspoon **salt**

2 cups **fresh blueberries**

GLAZE:

½ cup **confectioners' sugar**

¼ teaspoon **vanilla extract**

1½–2 teaspoons **warm water**

1

Preheat oven to 375°F.

Prepare the crumb topping first by cutting the butter into small pieces and placing it in a small bowl.

Using your fingers, mix the butter pieces with the granulated sugar, flour, and cinnamon. The mixture should be crumbly in texture.

Set aside.

2

Combine all the batter ingredients, except for the blueberries, in a mixing bowl or food processor fitted with a plastic blade and mix for 30 seconds.

Gently fold in the blueberries.

3

Pour the batter into the prepared pan and sprinkle the crumb topping over it.

Bake for 45 to 50 minutes, or until a cake tester inserted in the center comes out clean.

Mix together the glaze ingredients until smooth.

Drizzle over the warm cake.

Let cool on a wire rack, and then remove the cake from the pan.

Plum Crumb Cake

When plums are in season this cake is a dream: moist, and delicious, and impressive. If you prefer apples, just substitute the same amount of apples (peeled and sliced) and add 1 tablespoon of cinnamon.

10-inch springform pan, greased

½ cup **butter**, softened

¾ cup **granulated sugar**

1 small **egg**

1 tablespoon **milk**

2 cups **all-purpose flour**

2 teaspoons **baking powder**

2–3 tablespoons **jam** (strawberry, apricot, plum, or orange)

1 pound **fresh red plums**, sliced

1 tablespoon **brown sugar**

1

In a mixing bowl, combine the butter, granulated sugar, egg, milk, flour, and baking powder.
Transfer three quarters of the batter to the prepared pan and press down with your fingers. (Try coating your fingers with a bit of flour so that they don't get sticky.)

2

Shape the remaining batter into a ball and chill for 1 hour.

3

Preheat oven to 375°F.
Cover the batter in the pan with the jam and arrange the plum slices randomly around the top.
Sprinkle with the brown sugar.

4

Remove the chilled batter from the refrigerator and coarsely grate it over the plums.
Bake for 1 hour, or until golden.

Summer Plum Cake

So little work, so few ingredients—for such luscious results! This is the perfect cake for a lazy summer day.

10-inch springform pan, greased

$1/2$ cup plus $1/8$ cup **sugar**

$1/2$ cup **butter**, room temperature

3 large **eggs**, room temperature

1 cup **all-purpose flour**

1 teaspoon **baking powder**

grated **peel** of **1 lemon**

20 **Santa Rosa plums**, halved and pitted

$1/2$ tablespoon **cinnamon**

1

Preheat oven to 350°F.
In a mixing bowl, beat $1/2$ cup sugar with the butter.
Add the eggs, one at a time, mixing well after each addition.
Add the flour, baking powder, and grated lemon peel; mix well.
Pour the batter into the prepared pan.

2

Cover the batter with the halved plums (if very large, cut into quarters), cut side down, pressing into the dough with your fingers.

3

In a small bowl, combine the remaining $1/8$ cup sugar with the cinnamon and sprinkle over the plums.
Bake for 45 minutes, or until the cake starts to turn brown.
Serve warm or cold. (Store in refrigerator.)

Apricot Cake

A wonderful, light, fruity treat for a hot summer day. You can make a variety of this cake by substituting the apricots with plums or any other small fruit with a similar soft, juicy texture. If fresh apricots are not available, use a 30-ounce can of apricot halves and drain them well.

11¾ x 9¼ x 1½-inch pan, greased

3 large **eggs**, room temperature

1 cup **sugar**

1 teaspoon **vanilla extract**

⅓ cup **vegetable oil**

1¼ cups **all-purpose flour**

1¼ teaspoons **baking powder**

8 **fresh apricots**, pitted and halved

2 tablespoons **brown sugar**

1

Preheat oven to 350°F.

In a mixing bowl combine the eggs, sugar, vanilla, oil, flour, and baking powder and beat well.

Pour the batter into the prepared pan and arrange the apricots, cut side down, on top of the batter.

2

Sprinkle with brown sugar and bake for 45 minutes, or until golden.

Peach Cake

When you crave a piece of cake but aren't in the mood to fuss, this is the perfect solution. Just toss all the ingredients together and bake, then revel in this cake's marvelous maze of flavor and texture: nutty crunch, fluffy sweetness, juicy fullness . . . this cake has something for everyone!

8 1/2 x 4 1/2 x 2 3/4-inch loaf **pan**, greased

1 (15-ounce) **can whole peaches**, drained, with liquid set aside

1 1/2 cups **all-purpose flour**

1 1/2 teaspoons **baking powder**

1/4 teaspoon **salt**

3/4 cup **granulated sugar**

1/4 cup **brown sugar**

1/2 cup **vegetable oil**

1/4 cup **liquid from drained peaches**

1 teaspoon **vanilla extract**

2 small **eggs**, room temperature

1/2 cup chopped **walnuts**

1

Preheat oven to 350°F.

Cut the peaches into quarters. Combine all the ingredients in a mixer fitted with the dough hook (so that the peaches are not smashed) and mix to form batter.

2

Pour the batter into the prepared pan and bake for 50 minutes, or until golden.

Grape Cake

Believe it or not, grapes make a great cake!

---

10 ½-inch springform pan, greased

DOUGH:

²⁄₃ cup **granulated sugar**

1 cup **butter**, room temperature

2½ cups **all-purpose flour**

2 large **eggs**

grated **peel** of **1 lemon**

2 teaspoons **vanilla extract**

FILLING:

½ cup **butter**, room temperature

1 cup **confectioners' sugar**

1 teaspoon **vanilla extract**

grated **peel** of **1 lemon**

2 large **eggs** plus **1 egg yolk**

½ cup **all-purpose flour**

1 teaspoon **baking powder**

1 pound **seedless green** or **purple grapes**

sliced almonds, for decoration

1

In a mixer or food processor fitted with the steel blade, mix all the dough ingredients until well blended. Chill for 4 hours.

2

Preheat oven to 375°F.
Prepare the filling by beating together the butter and confectioners' sugar.
Gradually add the vanilla, grated lemon peel, eggs and egg yolk.
Fold in the flour and baking powder.

3

On a clean, floured work surface, using a floured rolling pin, roll out the dough to a circle wider than the diameter of the pan and with a thickness of ¹/₈ inch. Cover the bottom and sides of the pan with the dough.
Pour in half the filling, scatter half the grapes on top, cover with the remaining filling, then the remaining grapes.

4

Bake for 20 minutes, or until golden.
Remove from oven and scatter the almonds around the edge of the cake.

Assorted
Cakes

Pecan Meringue Cake

This cake is a wonderful addition to a party. You can cut it into individual squares and serve them in little paper cups. Feel free to substitute almonds for some of the pecans if you like.

---

13 x 9 x 2-inch cake pan, greased

1 cup **butter**, room temperature

4 large **eggs**, separated, room temperature

1 cup **all-purpose flour**

1 teaspoon **baking powder**

3 tablespoons **apricot jelly** (or any other flavor)

1 cup **pecans**, chopped

3/4 cup **sugar**

1

Preheat oven to 350°F.

In a mixer, combine the butter, egg yolks, flour, and baking powder.

Press onto the bottom of the greased pan.

Cover the batter with the apricot jelly and sprinkle with the nuts.

2

Beat the egg whites until they form soft peaks.

Gradually add the sugar, 1 tablespoon at a time, beating well after each addition. Stop beating when stiff peaks form.

Spread the meringue mixture on top of the jelly layer.

Don't worry about flattening out the meringue. It looks wonderful when the peaks bake.

3

Bake for 45 minutes, or until the meringue turns golden.

Marble Cake

Even though we all know how it's made, there's still something wondrously delightful about the swirling marble cake. This is a basic recipe that guarantees you moist, fluffy results every time. By mistake, this cake was once made with almond extract instead of vanilla—and the results were positively amazing. Be sure to try both.

10½ x 5½ x 2½-inch loaf **pan**, greased and floured

1 cup **butter**, room temperature

grated **peel** of **1** lemon

4 large **eggs**, room temperature

1½ cups **sugar**

1 teaspoon **vanilla** or **almond extract**

1½ cups **all-purpose flour**

1½ teaspoons **baking powder**

3 tablespoons **unsweetened cocoa**

1

Preheat oven to 350°F.

In a food processor fitted with the steel blade, mix everything except the cocoa for 2 minutes.

Pour half of the batter into the prepared pan.

Add the cocoa to the remaining batter and mix for less than a minute.

Pour over the first layer.

2

Bake for 35 to 45 minutes, or until a cake tester inserted in the center comes out clean.

Mocha Cream and Hazelnut Bars

This delicious cake can easily be cut into squares, so if you have company coming, don't hesitate. Easy to make and even easier to serve with each cake square in its own paper cup arranged on a platter.

Makes 30 squares

13 x 9 x 2½-inch pan, greased

1 cup **butter**, room temperature

1 cup **sugar**

2 cups **all-purpose flour**

2 teaspoons **baking powder**

2 large **egg yolks**

2 cups plain (not roasted) **hazelnuts** (can still have skins)

1 cup **whipping cream**

2 teaspoons **instant coffee powder**

2 tablespoons **sugar**

1
Preheat oven to 350°F.
In a food processor fitted with the steel blade, combine the butter, sugar, flour, baking powder, egg yolks, and hazelnuts and process until just mixed. (Don't overmix.)

2
Transfer the mixture to the prepared pan and press down.
Bake for 20 minutes, or until the crust browns.
Remove from oven and cut away a 3-inch wide strip of cake, lengthwise. (This will be used for crumbs at the end.) Let cool.

3
Beat the cream until it forms soft peaks. Reduce the speed of the mixer and add the coffee powder and sugar, 1 rounded teaspoon at a time, beating after each addition. Cover the cake with the cream.

4
Using your fingers, crumble the cake strip and sprinkle over the cream. Cut the cake into 2½-inch squares and refrigerate until ready to use. Serve in paper cups.

Semolina Cake

Middle Eastern in origin, this wonderful cake is especially moist because it's drizzled with syrup. It's incredibly delicious and perfect for a large crowd. You can bake it on your oven tray and cut it into individual squares.

approximately **12 x 16½-inch** baking sheet, greased

BATTER:

1½ cups **semolina flour**

1 cup **sugar**

1 cup **whipping cream**

1 cup **sour cream**

1 cup **shredded dried coconut**

2 teaspoons **baking powder**

3 large **eggs**, room temperature

½ cup **all-purpose flour**

SYRUP:

2 cups **sugar**

2¼ cups **water**

coconut, for decorating

1

Preheat oven to 350°F.

Mix all the batter ingredients together.

Pour into prepared pan and bake for 20 minutes, or until a cake tester inserted in the center comes out clean.

2

In a saucepan over medium heat, combine the 2 cups of sugar and $2^1/4$ cups of water for the syrup and bring to a boil.

Remove from heat and pour the syrup over the warm cake.

Let cool.

3

Sprinkle the cake with coconut, cut into squares, and place each piece in an individual paper cup.

Keep leftovers (if there are any) in the refrigerator.

Cinnamon Cake

This is the ultimate comfort cake. It fills the house with a wonderful welcoming aroma that seems to draw big and small from every room to the kitchen. Try it instead of cinnamon rolls for breakfast, smeared with butter at coffee or tea, or as a warm, cozy Christmas specialty served with eggnog.

9½ x 5½ x 3¼-inch loaf **pan**, greased

BATTER:

1½ cups **all-purpose flour**

1½ teaspoons **baking powder**

1 cup **granulated sugar**

½ cup **butter**, melted and cooled

¼ cup **milk**

2 large **eggs**, room temperature

TOPPING:

⅓ cup **brown sugar**

2 teaspoons **cinnamon**

¼ cup **butter**, cut into little cubes

1

Preheat oven to 350°F.

Sift together the flour and baking powder.

In a mixing bowl or food processor fitted with the steel blade, blend the flour mixture and granulated sugar.

With the mixer running, add the butter, milk, and eggs; beat until blended.

Pour batter into the prepared pan.

2

Mix the brown sugar and cinnamon for the topping and sprinkle over the batter.

Scatter the butter cubes over the sugar and cinnamon mixture. Bake for 40 minutes, or until a cake tester inserted in the center comes out clean.

Dutch Honey Cake

This old family favorite brings both sweet and spice to the table. Though it originated in Portugal, honey cake became a classic treat in Holland, where the Dutch love to slice it thin and slather it with butter at breakfast. If covered with aluminum foil, it can keep for two weeks— and only gets better with time.

---

2 (9 x 5½ x 3¼-inch) loaf pans, greased and floured

1¼ cups **sugar**

¾ cup **Earl Grey tea** (room temperature)

½ cup **canola oil**

1 cup **honey** (preferably eucalyptus or avocado)

2 large **eggs**, room temperature

2½ cups **all-purpose flour**

2½ level teaspoons **baking powder**

pinch of **black pepper**

pinch of **ground nutmeg**

1 heaping teaspoon **cinnamon**

1 teaspoon **ground ginger**

1 cup **walnut halves**

1

Preheat oven to 350°F.
Mix together all the ingredients except for the walnuts and blend well.
Stir in the walnut halves.

2

Pour the batter into the prepared pans and bake for 35 to 40 minutes, or until a cake tester inserted in the center comes out clean.

Lemon and Sour Cream Surprise

A buttery flavor combined with lemon and sour cream makes this a moist, yummy choice for any occasion. Serve it with whipped cream and fresh berries or as is. For a wonderful brunch treat, try toasting the slices and serving them with butter and jam.

10-inch bundt or **turk's-hat pan** or, greased and floured

3 cups **all-purpose flour**

1²⁄₃ cups **granulated sugar**

3 teaspoons **baking powder**

pinch of **salt**

¾ cup **sour cream**

¼ cup **milk**

3 large **eggs**, room temperature

2 large **egg yolks**

grated **peel** of **1 lemon**

1 teaspoon **vanilla extract**

1¼ cups **butter**, room temperature

confectioners' sugar, for decorating

1

Preheat oven to 350°F.

Sift the flour, granulated sugar, baking powder, and salt into the bowl of an electric mixer. In another medium-size bowl, whisk the sour cream, milk, whole eggs, egg yolks, lemon peel, and vanilla extract until well-blended.

2

Alternately add half the egg mixture and all the softened butter in small portions to the dry ingredients, beating at low speed just until blended. Increase the speed to high and beat 1 minute more. (Do not overmix.)

Add the remaining egg mixture and beat at medium-high speed until the batter is fluffy and smooth.

3

Transfer the batter to the prepared pan.

Bake for 50 to 60 minutes, or until the cake starts to brown and pull away from the pan sides, and a cake tester inserted in the center comes out clean.

Transfer to a wire rack to cool.

Remove from pan and sprinkle with confectioners' sugar sifted through a fine-mesh sieve.

Classic Butter Cake

Who doesn't love the subtle sweetness and golden glow of the beloved butter cake? This beautiful and delicious favorite is classy enough for formal occasions yet simple enough for breakfast at home. For a unique and colorful presentation, sprinkle with powdered sugar and garnish with strawberries, blueberries, or a dollop of whipped cream.

10-inch springform pan or **2 (9½ x 5½ x 3¼-inch) loaf pans**, greased

1 cup **butter**, room temperature

grated **peel** of **1 lemon**

4 large **eggs**, room temperature

1½ cups **sugar**

1 tablespoon **vanilla extract**

1½ cups **self-rising flour**

1

Preheat oven to 350°F.
Combine all the ingredients in a mixing bowl and mix well.

2

Pour the batter into the prepared pan(s).
Bake for 45 minutes, or until golden and a cake tester inserted in the center comes out clean.

German Coffee Cake

10½-inch springform pan,
greased

BATTER:

4 large **eggs**

2 teaspoons **vanilla extract**

2 cups **granulated sugar**

2 cups **all-purpose flour**

2 teaspoons **baking powder**

dash of **salt**

2 tablespoons **butter**

1 cup **milk**

TOPPING:

3 tablespoons **butter**

3 tablespoons **brown sugar**

2 tablespoons **sour cream**

½ cup **chopped pecans** or
flaked coconut

1

Preheat oven to 350°F.

In a mixing bowl, beat the eggs and vanilla together, then add the granulated sugar, flour, baking powder, and salt.

2

In a small saucepan over medium heat, mix together the butter and milk. When the butter has melted, remove the mixture from the heat and add it to the batter. (The batter will be very runny.) Mix well.

Pour the batter into the prepared pan and bake for 35 minutes or until golden and a cake tester inserted in the center comes out clean.

3

Preheat the broiler.

Prepare the topping by heating the butter and brown sugar in a saucepan over medium heat until melted.

Remove from heat and stir in the sour cream and pecans or coconut.

4

While the cake is still warm, cover with the topping and place under the broiler for a few minutes until it starts to bubble. Remove from oven and let cool.

Jelly Roll

Similar to cookies, these jelly rolls look very festive and last a long time if stored in a tin or glass container. They also make a lovely hostess gift. The dough must be prepared in advance.

---

18 x 13-inch nonstick pan, lined with parchment or baking paper

3 cups **all-purpose flour**

3 teaspoons **baking powder**

1 cup **butter**, room temperature

1 large **egg**, room temperature

¼ cup **fresh orange juice**

1 cup **jam** (strawberry, apricot, or orange)

1 cup **chopped walnuts**

confectioners' sugar, for decoration

1

In a mixer or food processor fitted with the steel blade, mix together the flour, baking powder, butter, egg, and orange juice until it forms a ball.
Cover with plastic food wrap and chill overnight.

2

Preheat oven to 350°F.
Remove dough from refrigerator and let stand for 10 minutes.
With a floured rolling pin on a clean, floured surface, roll out the dough to a rectangle measuring 11½ by 8½ inches.
Slice the dough into 3 long strips.

3

Spread each strip with one third of the jam, sprinkle with the chopped walnuts, and roll up tightly. Place the rolls on the prepared pan and bake for 30 minutes, or until golden.

4

Remove from the oven and let cool.
Sift confectioners' sugar through a fine-mesh sieve over the rolls and cut into slices.

Zucchini Bread

A wonderful addition to a brunch, this delicious zucchini creation is called bread, but we know it's really cake. Chopped pecans add a nutty tenderness to the comforting flavor of cinnamon and sugar. And, of course, with plenty of green zucchini, it's not completely cheating to count this as one of your daily vegetable servings!

---

2 (8½ x 4½ x 3¼-inch) loaf pans, greased

3 cups **all-purpose flour**

¼ teaspoon **baking powder**

1 teaspoon **baking soda**

1 teaspoon **salt**

2 teaspoons **cinnamon**

2 cups **sugar**

1 cup **canola oil**

3 teaspoons **vanilla extract**

3 large **eggs**, beaten

2 cups **zucchini**, peeled and grated

1 cup **chopped pecans**

additional **pecan halves**, for decoration

1

Preheat oven to 350°F.

In a medium-size mixing bowl, sift together the flour, baking powder, baking soda, salt, and cinnamon.

2

In another mixing bowl, beat the sugar, oil, vanilla, and eggs, until blended.

Fold in the zucchini and pecans.

Add the dry ingredients and mix well.

Pour the batter into the greased pans, decorate with pecan halves, and bake for 1 hour.

Remove from oven and let cool.

Cookies

Melt-in-Your-Mouth Cookies

Makes about 45 cookies

2 large **baking sheets**, lined with **parchment paper** (or use silicone baking sheets)

1½ cups **butter**, room temperature

1 teaspoon **vanilla extract**

8 tablespoons granulated **sugar**

2½ cups **all-purpose flour**

2½ teaspoons **baking powder**

45 pecan halves, whole almonds, or whole hazelnuts

confectioners' sugar, for decoration

1

Preheat oven to 350°F.

In a food processor fitted with the steel blade, combine all the ingredients except the nuts and confectioners' sugar and process until dough is formed.

Shape small balls (about the size of a small plum) and place them 1 inch apart on the prepared baking sheets. (The balls of dough naturally flatten during the baking process, so there is no need to press down the raw dough.)

Press a nut into the center of each ball.

2

Bake for 20 minutes, or until golden brown. Remove from oven and set the baking sheets on a wire rack to cool.

(Do not touch the cookies while they are warm because they are very delicate and will crumble.)

When cool, sprinkle the cookies with confectioners' sugar sifted through a fine-mesh sieve.

Note: For variety, you may want to add chopped almonds to the batter itself. In this case, use ¹/2 cup chopped almonds and the last part of step 1. Follow the rest of the directions as given.

Almond Meringue Cookies

Easy to make, these elegant and delicious little cookies are perfect for serving with coffee or tea after the main dessert.

Makes about 45 cookies

18 x 13-inch pan (preferably nonstick), lined with **parchment paper**

14 ounces **sliced** or **slivered almonds**

2 large **egg whites**

1/2 cup **sugar**

1

Preheat oven to 260°F.

In a mixing bowl, combine all the ingredients using a large spoon. Scoop teaspoon-size portions of dough and use your finger to slide each one onto the prepared baking pan about 2 inches apart. (Don't fuss over perfect circles. The cookies are more fun when they decide on their own shape.)

2

Bake for 20 minutes, or until the cookies begin to turn golden brown. (Keep a close watch. The cookies have a tendency to burn quickly.)

Remove pan from oven and let cool on a wire rack.

(The cookies are still soft when they come out of the oven but harden as they cool.)

3

When completely cool, peel the cookies off the paper and store in an airtight container or tin can.

Sesame Cookies

These super easy and super fast treats bring authentic Middle Eastern flavor to the Western palate. Unlike anything else you've ever tried, they're mysteriously crispy and chewy at the same time. Their unusual balance of sweet and bitter makes them the perfect light snack to nibble on between meals, or to take as "car food" on family outings.

Makes about 55 cookies

18 x 13-inch pan (preferably nonstick), lined with **parchment paper**

1 pound **sesame seeds**

½ cup **vegetable oil**

1 cup **all-purpose flour**

1 teaspoon **baking powder**

1 cup **sugar**

2 large **eggs**, room temperature

1

Preheat oven to 350°F.
In a mixing bowl, combine all the ingredients using a large spoon. Scoop teaspoon-size portions of dough and use your finger to slide each one onto the prepared pan, about 1 inch apart.

2

Bake for 20 minutes, or until golden brown.
Let cool on the pan

Madeleines

These wonderful little cookies resemble a miniature sponge cake in the shape of a shell. Popularized by Marcel Proust in *Remembrance of Things Past*, they are incredibly easy to make and very impressive to serve. A sure hit with company and a perfect ending to a lovely meal.

Makes 12 cookies

Madeleine pan with 12 shell indentations, greased (or use silicone Madeleine pan)

5 heaping tablespoons **granulated sugar**

1 large **egg**

pinch of **salt**

¼ cup **butter**, melted and cooled

½ cup **all-purpose flour**

peel of **½ lemon**, grated

confectioners' sugar, for decorating

1

Preheat oven to 200°F.

In a mixer, beat together the granulated sugar, egg, and salt at medium speed until the mixture turns light yellow. Reduce the speed and alternately add the flour and the melted butter in small amounts, beating well after each addition.

Add the grated lemon peel and stir with a spoon.

2

Fill each shell form two thirds full with a spoonful of the batter, place in the preheated oven and bake for 5 minutes.

Raise the temperature to 400°F and bake for an additional 8 to 10 minutes.

When the Madeleines start to turn golden, remove the pan from the oven and flip it over so that the madeleines fall free onto a clean kitchen towel.

3

Let cool completely, then arrange on a serving plate.

Sprinkle with confectioners' sugar sifted through a fine-mesh sieve and serve.

Biscotti

A variation of traditional Italian biscotti, this version is light, crunchy, and laden with chocolate chips.

18 x 13-inch pan, lined with **parchment paper**

2 large **eggs**

1 cup **sugar**

2½ cups **all-purpose flour**

2½ teaspoons **baking powder**

1 cup **butter**, room temperature

1 cup **sliced almonds**

1 cup **walnuts**, coarsely chopped

½ cup **chocolate chips**

1

Preheat oven to 350°F.

In a mixing bowl, beat the eggs and sugar until the mixture turns light yellow. Combine one half the flour with the baking powder. Divide the flour mixture in half and incorporate, alternately with the butter, beating well after each addition.

In another bowl, mix the remaining flour with the almonds, walnuts, and chocolate chips. Combine this mixture with the first one and beat at low speed until well blended.

2

Flour your hands (the dough will be very sticky) and divide the dough into three loaf shapes. Place the 3 loaves on the prepared pan. (Don't worry if they look a bit messy. They will look better as they bake.) Using a knife, make diagonal slits (not too deep) 1½ inches apart along the length of each loaf. These slits form the outline for the slices.

3

Bake for 50 to 60 minutes, or until well browned.

Turn off oven and remove pan. Cut the loaves along the slit lines, but keep them on the pan. Return to oven (it must be turned off!) and leave there for several hours or overnight. (This step is critical since it enables the biscotti to harden.)

Remove from oven and store in a tin or glass container.

Tahini Cookies

This cookie is a Mediterranean-inspired treat. Pure sesame paste can be purchased in Middle Eastern and speciality food shops.

Makes about 70 cookies

large **baking sheet**, lined with **parchment paper**

3 cups **all-purpose flour**

1 cup **butter**, room temperature

1 cup **sugar**

1 cup **pure tahini** (unseasoned sesame paste)

1

Preheat oven to 350°F.

In a mixing bowl or food processor fitted with the steel blade, combine all the ingredients and process until dough is formed. Shape the dough into 3/4-inch balls and place them 1 inch apart on the prepared baking sheet.

2

Bake for 25 to 30 minutes, or until the cookies start to turn golden.

(Watch closely so they don't brown.)

Remove baking sheet from oven and let cool for 5 minutes on wire rack.

Loosen each cookie with a rubber spatula to prevent sticking and continue cooling.

When completely cooled, remove from pan and store in an airtight container.

Irresistible Butter Cookies

These cookies are a hit anytime, anyplace. They're adorable placed next to a cup of coffee or tea, and absolutely irresistible dipped in hot chocolate. They require incredibly short preparation time and minimal effort, and it's a good thing, too, because you'll have to make more before you know it.

Makes about 70 small cookies

2 baking sheets, lined with **parchment paper**

1¾ cups **butter**, room temperature

3½ cups **all-purpose flour**

1 cup **confectioners' sugar**

1

Preheat oven to 350°F.

In a food processor fitted with a steel blade, combine all the ingredients and process until dough is formed.

Shape ³/₄-inch balls (the width of a nickel) and place them 1 inch apart on the prepared baking sheets.

2

Bake for 15 minutes.

The cookies are ready when they are light in color with slightly golden edges.

Remove baking sheets from oven and let cool on a wire rack.

Store in an airtight container.

Butter Pecan Cookies

Tired of the same old pecan pie? Well, there's more than one way to use this Southern autumn specialty. These cookies have far less sugar than the traditional pie, and their delightfully crumbly texture and buttery flavor are a refreshing change from that heavy, syrupy classic. A truly American cookie!

Makes about 40 cookies

18 x 13-inch pan, lined with **parchment paper**

½ cup **butter**, room temperature

4 tablespoons **granulated sugar**

1 teaspoon **vanilla extract**

1 cup **crushed pecans**

1 cup **all-purpose flour**

1 teaspoon **baking powder**

confectioners' sugar, for decoration

1

Preheat oven to 350°F.
In a mixing bowl or food processor fitted with the steel blade, combine all ingredients except the confectioners' sugar.
Beat or process for 3 minutes, or until the dough forms a ball.

2

Form ¾-inch balls and place them 1 inch apart on the prepared pan.
Bake for 15 to 20 minutes (and no more).
Remove pan from oven and let cool on wire rack.

3

While the cookies are still warm, sprinkle generously with confectioners' sugar sifted through a fine-mesh sieve.

Speculaas (Ginger Cookies)

Originally a Dutch creation, these popular cookies traditionally have pictures imprinted on them. They are fondly referred to as Santa Claus cookies and are very popular around the holidays. This is an easier version, with the cookies cut into diamond shapes.

Makes about 40 cookies

1 baking sheet, greased

1 cup **butter**, room temperature

1 cup **sugar**

2 cups **all-purpose flour**

1½ teaspoons **cinnamon**

1½ teaspoons **ginger**

½ teaspoon **ground cloves**

¼ teaspoon **ground allspice**

1

In a food processor fitted with the steel blade, combine all the ingredients and process until a dough is formed.

On a clean, floured surface with a floured rolling pin roll out the dough to a thickness of ⅛ inch.

Picking up the dough in pieces, cover the entire baking sheet. (You can transfer the dough straight from the mixing bowl to the tray by pushing down and shaping the dough with your fingers.) Chill for 1 hour.

2

Preheat oven to 350°F.

Remove the chilled dough from the refrigerator and bake for 15 minutes, or until golden.

Remove from oven and cut immediately into diamond shapes using a very sharp knife. (First cut lengthwise into 1-inch strips, then cut diagonally across the pan to create diamond shapes.)

Let cool for a few minutes on the sheet, then remove.

Store in an airtight container.

Scones & Muffins

Apple Muffins

Store-bought apple-cinnamon muffins can't compete with these fresh and fluffy morsels. Golden raisins add sweet, juicy spots of flavor to melting apples and lightly spicy cake. This is the perfect recipe when you have "nothing" in the pantry or just want a simple but special breakfast treat. You'll never go back to store-bought again!

Makes 12 muffins

12-cup muffin pan, greased

2 cups **all-purpose flour**

2 teaspoons **baking powder**

⅓ cup **sugar**

pinch of **salt**

1 tablespoon **cinnamon**

1 cup peeled and coarsely grated **Granny Smith apples** (approximately 2)

½ cup **golden raisins**

1 large **egg**

1 cup **milk**

2 ounces **butter**, room temperature

1

Preheat oven to 350°F.
In a mixing bowl, combine the flour, baking powder, sugar, salt, and cinnamon; whisk until blended.
Add the grated apples and raisins; stir to combine.

2

In another bowl, gently whisk the egg.
Add the milk and butter, whisking continuously.
Add this mixture to the flour and apple mixture and stir just enough to blend the ingredients together. (Do not overmix!)
Fill each muffin-pan cup-two thirds full with the batter.
Bake for 20 minutes, or until golden brown.

Simple Scones

A variation of the classic English scone, this is the ultimate treat for breakfast or afternoon tea. Best served slightly warm with butter and jam.

Makes 12 scones

12-cup muffin pan, greased

2 cups **all-purpose flour**

2 teaspoons **baking powder**

2 tablespoons **sugar**

pinch of **salt**

2 ounces **butter**, room temperature

1 large **egg**

¾ cup **milk**

2 tablespoons **currants** or **raisins**

1

Preheat oven to 400°F.

In a food processor fitted with the steel blade, combine the flour, baking powder, sugar, and salt and process for 1 minute.

Add the butter and process for another minute.

Add the egg and milk and process just until the mixture is well blended. (Do not overmix.)

Stir in the currents (or raisins).

2

Using a tablespoon to scoop the batter, fill the muffin-pan cups.

Bake for 20 minutes or until golden.

Remove and serve.

Serving suggestion: Line a wicker basket with a red-and-white checkered napkin, add the scones, and cover with another napkin to keep warm.

Cinnamon Popovers

There is nothing more wonderful than fresh-from-the-oven popovers for breakfast or brunch. They must be served warm because they have a tendency to collapse.

Makes 6 popovers in a popover pan (or 12 in a muffin pan)

popover or **muffin pan** (preferably nonstick), greased and floured

1/3 cup **butter**, room temperature, plus

1/3 cup **butter**, melted and cooled

1 cup **sugar**

1 large **egg**

1½ cups **all-purpose flour**

1½ teaspoons **baking powder**

pinch of **salt**

¼ teaspoon **ground nutmeg**

½ cup **milk**

1 teaspoon **cinnamon**

1

Preheat oven to 350°F.

In a mixer, combine the room-temperature butter, ¹/₂ cup of the sugar, and the egg.

In another bowl, combine the flour, baking powder, salt, and nutmeg. Add the flour mixture to the butter and egg mixture and beat well. Gradually add the milk while continuing to beat.

2

Using a tablespoon, scoop the batter into the pan, filling each muffin-pan cup three-quarters full.

Bake for 20 to 25 minutes, or until golden.

3

Pour the melted butter into a pan or large plate.

Combine the remaining ¹/₂ cup sugar with the cinnamon.

Remove the popovers from the oven, flip them out of the pan, and roll them first in the melted butter, then roll them in the cinnamon-sugar mixture and serve warm.

No-Bake
Cakes & Treats

Cookies-and-Cream Cake

Absolutely delicious . . . just don't think about the calories. This cake is best made two days in advance and kept in the refrigerator. It can easily be cut into individual squares.

10 x 11½-inch baking pan

2 packages **petit beurre** or **tea biscuits** (28 cookies)

2 cups **milk**

2 cups **whipping cream**

1 1.4-ounce package **instant vanilla pudding**

2 tablespoons **sugar**

1 14-ounce **can apricots,** drained

chopped pecans, for decorating

1

Dip 14 biscuits into 1 cup milk and line the bottom of the pan with them. Reserve milk.
In a mixing bowl, beat 1 cup of the whipping cream until it forms soft peaks. Add the pudding mix and remaining 1 cup milk and beat well. Spread the cream over the biscuits in the pan.

2

Cut the apricots in half (or quarters if very large). Distribute the pieces evenly over the cream.
Dip the remaining biscuits into the remaining milk and place them over the apricots.

3

Beat the remaining 1 cup whipping cream until it forms soft peaks. Gradually add the sugar and continue beating until stiff. Spread the cream over the layer of biscuits. Sprinkle with the pecans and cover the pan with plastic food wrap.
Refrigerate for two days. (If you can't wait, one day will do.)

Truffles

Who can resist these charming chocolate morsels? They are the perfect complement to a strong cup of espresso at the end of a wonderful meal. Elegant, impressive, and a great project to make with children.

Makes about 20 truffles

2½ ounces **butter**

10 ounces **bittersweet chocolate**

1 cup **whipping cream**

5 tablespoons **Amaretto, chocolate liqueur, or brandy**

cocoa powder, coconut, chopped almonds, for decorating

1

Combine the butter, chocolate, cream, and liqueur in a double-boiler and mix well. When the chocolate has completely melted, remove from heat and chill for at least 4 hours, until completely hardened.

2

Remove chocolate from refrigerator.
Coat your fingers with the cocoa powder and scoop out a teaspoonful of the chocolate mixture.
Roll each teaspoonful into a ball and coat with the cocoa powder, coconut, or chopped almonds.
If the chocolate starts to melt, put it in the freezer for several minutes until it hardens again and then continue with the coating process.

3

Place each ball in a miniature paper cup and then directly on a serving plate.
If you're ambitious, carefully pile them in a pyramid shape on a lovely glass cake stand.

Easy Tiramisu

This cake is so easy you may not want to admit it to friends.
Reminiscent of a tiramisu, the taste is amazing, so don't let its
simplicity fool you.

---

8 x 8 x 2-inch baking pan

40 ladyfingers (preferably the
long, crispy ones)

1 cup **strong coffee**, cooled

½ cup **strawberry jam**

1 cup **whipping cream**

2 teaspoons **sugar**

½ cup **unsalted peanuts**,
coarsely chopped

1

Dip 20 ladyfingers into the coffee and cover the bottom of the
pan with them. Reserve the coffee.

2

Using a spatula, carefully spread the jam over the layer of
ladyfingers, being careful not to crush them. (They will be very
soft after soaking up the coffee.)

3

In a mixing bowl, whip the cream until it forms soft peaks.
Gradually add the sugar and continue to beat until stiff.
Spread half of the cream mixture over the jam layer.

4

Dip the remaining ladyfingers into the remaining coffee and lay
them on top of the cream.
Cover with the remaining cream and sprinkle with chopped
peanuts.
Chill for several hours before serving.

Chocolate Tent Cake

Who would believe that such a fun and impressive cake is so incredibly easy to prepare? It makes a great birthday cake when decorated with M&M's or other individual candies.

---

36 petit beurre or **tea biscuits** (1½ packages)

FILLING:

1 cup **whipping cream**

1 (1.4-ounce) package **instant vanilla pudding**

1 cup **milk**

ICING:

8 ounces **bittersweet chocolate**

1 cup **whipping cream**

1

Sprinkle some drops of water over a clean work surface and then cover with a 12 x 12-inch sheet of aluminum foil. (The water helps keep the foil on the surface and prevents it from slipping.)

In a mixing bowl, beat the whipping cream until it forms soft peaks.

Gradually add the pudding mix and milk and continue to beat until stiff.

2

Arrange the biscuits in the center of the foil in 3 rows of 6 biscuits each. Using a spatula, spread half the filling onto the biscuits, cover with the remaining biscuits, then spread the rest of the filling. Place your hands under both long sides of the aluminum foil. Using the foil as an aid, lift up the 2 outer rows of cookies until their top edges touch one another to create a tent shape. Seal the foil on the top and chill for at least 4 hours.

3

Heat the chocolate in a double boiler until melted and smooth; remove from heat. Add the whipping cream and stir until well blended.

4

Remove the cake from the refrigerator, open the foil, and spread the chocolate icing on the "tent" using a spatula. Cut away the excess foil and chill until ready to use. When ready to serve, slice the tent with a sharp knife.

Date and Coconut Rolls

Make them, put them in the freezer, and keep them for months. A great treat for unexpected guests or for a hostess. Dates are available at Middle Eastern markets and specialty food shops; pressed dates are the ones that come in a block.

Makes 2 rolls

1 cup **margarine**

½ cup **sugar**

1 pound **dried dates**, pitted and pressed

1 large **egg**

1½ cups **petit beurre** or **tea biscuits**, coarsely ground

1 cup **pecans**, coarsely chopped

dried coconut flakes, for coating

1

Place the margarine and sugar in a saucepan and cook over medium heat until the margarine has melted.

Gradually add the dates and stir until blended.

Remove from heat (the mixture will be slightly separated) and immediately add the egg, stirring rapidly until well blended.

Stir in the biscuits and pecans.

2

Form the mixture into 2 long, tube-shaped rolls.

Roll each in the coconut, wrap in plastic food wrap, and freeze. The rolls keep for months in the freezer.

Fifteen minutes before serving, remove rolls from freezer and cut crosswise into slices with a very sharp knife.

Rice Krispies–Halvah Bites

These wonderful treats take about five minutes to prepare. More a candy than a cake, they are perfect for afternoon tea, a late-night snack, or an answer to that craving for "something sweet."

10 x 8-inch pan, greased

4 ounces **vanilla-flavored halvah**, crumbled

1/4 cup **margarine**

3 tablespoons **honey**

2 tablespoons **sugar**

1 teaspoon **instant coffee powder**

4 cups **Rice Krispies** cereal

1/4 cup **sesame seeds**

1

Combine the halvah, margarine, honey, sugar, and coffee powder in a saucepan and cook over medium heat, stirring occasionally for several minutes.

When the mixture comes together, remove from heat.

Add the Rice Krispies and mix well using a wooden spoon.

2

Spread the mixture out on the prepared pan using a spatula.

Put the sesame seeds in a dry skillet and toss over medium heat for a few minutes until they turn golden, then scatter them over the dough.

Chill for several hours.

When set, cut into $1^1/_2$ x $1^1/_2$-inch squares and serve in individual paper cups.

Savory
Delights

Mini Cheddar Croissants

When you're not in the mood for something sweet but still crave something from the oven, try these wonderful little croissants. Nigella seeds (also known as black onion seeds) are available at Middle Eastern and specialty food shops.

Makes 24 mini croissants

large **baking sheet**, lined with **parchment paper**

2½ cups **all-purpose flour**

2½ tablespoons **baking powder**

1 cup **plain yogurt** (preferably Greek)

1 cup **margarine**, room temperature

1½ cups grated **Cheddar cheese** (10 ounces)

1 **egg yolk**, mixed with 1 tablespoon **water,** for brushing

1 small package **nigella** or **sesame seeds**

1

In a food processor fitted with the steel blade, combine the flour, baking powder, yogurt, margarine, and cheese. Pulse until dough is formed. Shape the dough into a ball, cover with plastic food wrap, and chill for several hours.

2

Preheat oven to 400°F. Remove the dough from refrigerator and divide into four sections. Using a floured rolling pin on a floured work surface, flatten out each section into a circle about 6 to 7 inches in diameter and ⅛-inch thick. Cut across the circles in an X-shape, then slice each quarter into thirds, creating long, thin triangular pieces. Starting from the base and rolling toward the tip, form each triangle into a croissant shape.

3

Brush each croissant with the egg yolk and water mixture and gently sprinkle with nigella seeds to taste. Lay them out on the baking sheet and bake for 30 minutes, or until the croissants start to turn golden.

You may also place the sheet of unbaked croissants directly into the freezer. When they are completely frozen, transfer them to a plastic bag and freeze for several months. When you want to bake, just remove them from the bag and place them in a preheated oven.

Cheese Rolls

Dairy lovers won't be able to get enough of these delectable rolls. With two types of cheese and a generous helping of butter, you'll think heaven is in Wisconsin! They're even easier to make than a traditional buttermilk biscuit, and they fill the house with a far more rewarding—and irresistible—aroma.

Makes about 20 rolls

Baking sheet, lined with **parchment paper**

9 ounces **cream cheese**, room temperature

1 large **egg**

2½ cups **all-purpose flour**, sifted

2½ teaspoons **baking powder**

1 cup **butter**, room temperature

1 cup grated **Swiss cheese** (8 ounces)

dash of **salt**

dash of **sugar**

1

Place the cream cheese in a food processor fitted with the steel blade and process until whipped.
Mix in the remaining ingredients.
Form the dough into a ball, wrap in plastic food wrap, and chill for 2 hours.

2

Preheat oven to 350°F.
Form the dough into about 20 small balls and arrange them on the baking sheet, leaving about ½ inch between each one.
Bake for 40 minutes, or until golden.
Serve warm.

Goat Cheese Roulade

This unique dough combines the creaminess of cheese with the crunchiness of nuts to produce a winning pastry all by itself. Fill it with . . . more cheese (what else?), and you can serve it as a hearty meal any time of day. Make sure you keep an eye on it, though—this is one roulade that rolls out of sight very fast!

baking sheet, lined with **parchment paper**

PASTRY:

½ cup (4 ounces) **goat cheese**, crumbled

1 tablespoon **cream cheese**

½ cup **all-purpose flour**

3 tablespoons **sesame seeds**

⅓ cup **pecans**, finely chopped

¼ cup **butter**, room temperature

1 tablespoon **sour cream**

salt & pepper to taste

FILLING:

2 (4-ounce) **goat cheese** rolls

1

In a food processor fitted with the steel blade, combine all the pastry ingredients and process until smooth.

Form the dough into a ball, wrap in plastic food wrap, and chill for 1 hour.

Remove from refrigerator and knead slightly with your hands.

2

Preheat oven to 350°F.

Using a floured rolling pin on a clean, floured surface, roll the dough into a rectangle measuring 10 x 6 inches.

Place the goat cheese rolls lengthwise down the center of the rectangle, end-to-end.

Starting at one long end, roll up the dough and place it on the prepared baking sheet.

Bake for 20 minutes, or until the roulade starts to turn golden.

Before serving, cut the roll crosswise into slices.

Beer Bread

So easy to make, this bread will fill your home with a wonderful aroma. Delicious as is or serve as toast with cream cheese or butter. You might even want to try it cut into small pieces, spread with goat cheese, and garnished with an arugula leaf and half a purple grape.

2 (8½ x 4½ x 2¾-inch) loaf **pans**, greased

5 cups **all-purpose flour**

5 teaspoons **baking powder**

4 cups **beer**

3 tablespoons **sugar**

1 teaspoon **salt**

5 tablespoons halved **walnuts** (or **sunflower seeds**)

1 **egg white**, lightly beaten, for brushing

1

Preheat oven to 350°F.

In a mixing bowl, combine all the ingredients except the egg white and stir until blended.

Divide the batter between the 2 loaf pans and smooth the tops with a spatula.

Brush the tops with the egg white.

2

Bake for 45 minutes, or until the loaves turn golden.

Index